CADILLAC

STANDARD OF THE WORLD

by
SHIRLEY HAINES
and
HARRY HAINES

THE ROURKE CORPORATION, INC.
Vero Beach, FL 32964

CREDITS

The authors and publisher wish to thank Cadillac Motor Car Division for invaluable assistance in compiling the technical information for this book. Special thanks are due Vince Muniga and Jerry Norkooli for locating the photographs, all of which were obtained from Cadillac. Special appreciation is owed to Bobby Railsback and Jim Davis of the Gene Messer Agency (Cadillac's dealer in Amarillo, Texas) for their continuous help, guidance and encouragement.

© 1993 The Rourke Corporation, Inc.

Library of Congress Cataloging-in-Publication Data

Haines, Shirley, 1935-
    Cadillac: standard of the world / by Shirley and Harry Haines.
      p. cm. – (Car classics)
    Includes index.
    Summary: Gives a brief history of the Cadillac automobile and describes its special features and some classic models.
    ISBN 0-86593-252-2
    1. Cadillac automobile – History – Juvenile literature.
[1. Cadillac automobile.] I. Haines, Harry, 1932-   . II. Title.
III. Series: Car classics (Vero Beach, Fla.)
TL215.C27H35 1993
629.222'2 – dc20   92-42305
                                   CIP
                                   AC

Printed in the USA

FY 97 Regular BOE, Garrett Books 10/9/96

CONTENTS

1. Always the Best 4

2. The Beginning 6

3. The Standard of the World 8

4. The Car Without a Crank 10

5. The V-16 Cadillac 12

6. Before and After World War II 14

7. Cars of the '50s 16

8. Tail Fins 18

9. Cadillac, 1960-90 20

10. Allanté 22

11. Cadillac Today: De Ville,
    Sixty Special, Fleetwood 24

12. Cadillac Today: Seville and Eldorado 26

13. Future Cadillacs 28

14. Cadillac: Important Dates 30

    Glossary 31

    Index 32

CHAPTER 1

ALWAYS THE BEST

Cadillac is more than an automobile. It is a status symbol. And to many Americans, the owning of a Cadillac means, "I have achieved," or "I am a success."

The word, "Cadillac," has become a synonym for wealth or prosperity. If something is "the Cadillac" of its class, it is the best or it has the highest qualities of luxury and elegance. "Cadillac Style" means living in comfort and affluence.

A 1993 Cadillac Seville STS. This luxury sports sedan was the first automobile to win every leading automotive magazine award.

Other top-of-the-line car names do not have the same implications. When talking about a piece of furniture or a particular tool that is the best model, people don't say, "It's the Studebaker of sofas" or "It is the Edsel of electric saws."

Name recognition for quality does not suddenly appear. It trickles into our culture in tiny bits, in ways that are all but invisible. Why has the name "Cadillac" developed its image for quality? It is because Cadillac cars have, for almost a hundred years, always been the best.

Cadillac is the only car company to win the Malcolm Baldrige National Quality Award.

One of the world's best-known symbols is the coat of arms of Le Sieur Antoine de la Mothe Cadillac. It was adopted for use on Cadillac motorcars in 1905 and registered as a trademark on August 7, 1906. Cadillac was born in Gascony, France in 1658. His heroic adventures as an American explorer were climaxed by the founding of Detroit in 1701.

THE BEGINNING

Henry Martyn Leland, the founder of the Cadillac Automobile Company, was born in Vermont in 1843. He was 59 years old when he built his first car and named it after the French explorer who founded Detroit in about 1701.

In 1902 Cadillac built three cars. They were designed by Henry Ford, who at that time was chief engineer for the struggling little company. During Cadillac's first year, an argument developed between these two men named Henry that became one of the most famous controversies in the history of the automobile. Henry Leland wanted to build cars of the highest quality. Henry Ford wanted to build cars at the lowest cost. The dispute was settled when Ford left shortly thereafter to found his own company.

Cadillac production began in March, 1903. Within the next year the company had produced 1,895 cars. By

The founder of Cadillac, Henry Martyn Leland, is shown here posing with his personal car, a 1905 model that he drove for many years. This picture was taken in 1930 when Leland was age 87.

October, 1905, Cadillac was the largest car maker in the world and was producing 4,000 machines a year.

Henry Leland made Cadillac's manufacturing famous for its precise measurements. In a time when most cars were handmade and there was little or no attention given to standardization of parts, Cadillac engines were accurate to the nearest 1/1,000 of an inch. As a result, the cars were recognized for their quality and reliability. The advertising slogan was, "When you buy a Cadillac you buy a round trip."

A 1902 Cadillac Runabout, the company's first production car. The passengers sat very high and the ride was hard. There were no instruments, and weather protection was zero.

Model	1902 Runabout
Period of production	1902
Number of cylinders	1
Horsepower @ rpm	10 @ 900
Gearbox	2-speed
Maximum speed	30 mph
Units produced	3

CHAPTER 3

THE STANDARD OF THE WORLD

In 1908 a contest was held in London, England, under the auspices of the Royal Automobile Club. It was a standardization test to check the interchangeability of parts. The winner would be awarded the Dewar Trophy. At that time the "Dewar" was considered the Nobel Prize of the automobile world and was awarded annually to the company making the most important advancement in car design and manufacturing.

The three 1908 Cadillacs at the Dewar Trophy "Test" in London, England.

The rules were very strict. A company had to submit three cars, take them completely apart, mix up the parts, randomly reassemble the parts into three totally new cars, and finish by running a 500-mile race to show that the cars would really work. In a time when almost all cars were made by hand and with little or no standardization, the test seemed impossible. Only one company entered: Cadillac. To everyone's surprise, all three cars completed the test successfully and on March 11, 1908, Cadillac was awarded the trophy.

All London papers treated it as a major news event and devoted huge coverage to the details. Over and over the phrase, "Standard of the World," was used to describe Cadillac's preciseness of engineering.

Today, Cadillac still uses the phrase as their company slogan.

In order to prove that it was possible to have interchangeable parts, the three cars were completely disassembled.

Model	Thirty
Period of production	1908/09
Number of cylinders	4
Horsepower	25.6
Gearbox	3-speed
Maximum speed	50 mph
Units produced	5,902

CHAPTER 4

THE CAR WITHOUT A CRANK

A 1912 Cadillac five-passenger touring car, the car that had no crank. It won the Dewar Trophy for Cadillac a second time.

The 1912 Cadillac marked a turning point in the history of the automobile. For the first time a motor car had a total electrical system. While the electrical ignition was a significant improvement over the old magneto used in contemporary cars – and the generator, rechargeable battery and electrical lights were also hailed as wonderful advancements – it was the electric self-starter that changed the course of automotive manufacturing. Furthermore, it established Cadillac again as the "Standard of the World" for innovation and design excellence.

The electric self-starter was developed in a tiny workshop in Dayton, Ohio by Charles F. Kettering. Mr. Kettering called his little business the "Dayton Engineering Laboratories Company," or DELCO for short. In the 1920s, "DELCO" became a synonym for "automotive electronics," and Charles Kettering became one of the engineering leaders at Cadillac.

Model	Thirty
Period of production	1912/13
Number of cylinders	4
Capacity (cubic inches)	365.8
Horsepower	48.7
Gearbox	3-speed
Maximum speed	60 mph (estimated)
Units produced	14,000
List price	$1,800

"The Car Without a Crank" was recognized by the Royal Automobile Club of London, England, for another Dewar Trophy in 1913. Never before in the history of the RAC had an automobile received the trophy a second time.

The Dayton Engineering Laboratories Company where Charles F. Kettering developed the first successful electric automobile starter. The company became famous as a division of General Motors under the name, "DELCO."

CHAPTER 5

THE V-16 CADILLAC

In 1926 work began on a new engine that was intended to give Cadillac the leadership position in the American luxury car market. At the time work on the huge engine was beginning, Cadillac was only one of a number of luxury cars that were competing for sales to America's aristocracy. Packard, Pierce-Arrow, Lincoln, Franklin and Marmon were all aiming for sales to the wealthy.

Ironically, the first V-16 Cadillac was introduced in December, 1929, just a few short weeks after the famous stock market crash that signaled the beginning of the Great Depression. But the severity of the nation's economic problems were not yet fully realized, and the new car sold well. By April, 1930, over 1,000 V-16s had been built. The total production for 1930 of 2,887 cars was nothing short of remarkable, considering the rapidly deteriorating economic situation in the United States. After 1931 production dropped to a trickle, and beyond 1933 the V-16 was built only for "special orders."

The V-16 was attacked by the American writer Thorstein Veblen. At the height of the Great Depression he used it as an example to coin the phrase, "conspicuous consumption."

Cadillac's last V-16 came off the line in 1940. Today these cars are among the most highly prized by car collectors.

Model	452/452A
Period of production	1930/31
Number of cylinders	16
Capacity (cubic inches)	452
Horsepower @ rpm	165 @ 3400
Gearbox	3-speed
Maximum speed	100 mph
Units produced	3,251
List price	$5,350 to $9,200

A 1931 V-16 Sport Phaeton Cadillac. This classic car is representative of the biggest cars of the 1920s and 1930s. The so-called "Golden Age" of large expensive automobiles was heavily influenced by automotive designers like Cadillac's Harley Earle. Up until this time cars were designed by engineers.

CHAPTER 6

BEFORE AND AFTER WORLD WAR II

During the depths of the Great Depression, automobile manufacturing suffered as much if not more than any other industry. Famous cars like Duesenberg, Pierce-Arrow, Auburn, Marmon and Peerless were quietly discontinued. Few people realize that Cadillac might have been dropped, had it not been supported by Chevrolet and Pontiac sales.

Economic conditions improved gradually and by 1941 Cadillac production reached a new high with 29,250 cars. One of the "siren" glamour cars of the early 1940s was the Cadillac four-door convertible. It was one of the major symbols of the Jazz Era. During World War II, the hope of coming home to one of these cars kept many a GI, sailor and officer going.

A 1941 four-door convertible. The famed "eggcrate" grill became a Cadillac hallmark and is still used on some models in the 1990s.

Never in the history of the motor car has there been any sales period like the late 1940s. Following the war American drivers would buy anything with four wheels and an engine. It is not surprising that most new car offerings in the first few years of postwar production were warmed-over prewar designs. Advertisers, including Cadillac, tried to turn this negative into a positive. Quoting directly from the 1946 showroom brochure, we learn the following: "In fact, we improved the Cadillac engine and transmission more in four years of war than would have been possible in four years of peace. You'll learn in the first mile, why we say, from Victory on the Battlefield to Victory on the Highway."

A 1946 Fleetwood five-passenger touring sedan. Cadillac offered very conservative prewar carryover models in 1946, '47 and '48.

Model	1946 Fleetwood Series 75
Number of cylinders	V-8
Capacity (cubic inches)	346
Horsepower @ rpm	150 @ 3400
Transmission	3-speed manual or Hydra-matic
Maximum speed	95 mph
Acceleration 0-60 mph	16 seconds
Units produced	1,292 (Fleetwood only)
List price	$4,095

CHAPTER 7

CARS OF THE '50s

In 1949 Cadillac had new postwar styling and a new "hot" V-8 engine. *Motor Trend* selected it the "Car of the Year." Later, this same magazine called Cadillac's V-8 "the engine an industry adopted."

Chicago car enthusiast, Edward Gaylord, reported the following:

> The 1950 Cadillac Series 61 with 160 hp V-8 and 3-speed standard shift was the fastest car made in the United States and perhaps the fastest accelerating stock car in the world. I owned one and a new Jaguar XK-120 at the time, and the Cadillac was the fastest car up to about 90 mph. My Cadillac set what was then a stock car record at the original quarter-mile drag races in Santa Ana, California.

Cadillac innovations in the '50s included the pillarless four-door hardtop sedan, cruise-control, high-pressure engine cooling, quad headlights, and two-speaker radio with automatic signal-seeking tuner.

Below: A 1959 Eldorado Biarritz Convertible. This was Cadillac at its biggest with tail fins at the max.

*Above: A 1949 Series 62
Cadillac Convertible, the first
of the "new" design to appear
after World War II.*

Dan Cordtez, writing in the *Wall Street Journal*, asked the rhetorical question, "Why is Cadillac so successful?" His answer: "Prestige, genuine comfort and luxury, excellent quality of construction, good performance, and a very good resale value."

The *WSJ* didn't talk about image or the intangible qualities that touch the hearts of men and women and inspire a song. Cadillac's image was so strong it became the basis of a Broadway stage hit, *The Solid Gold Cadillac*.

Model	1949 Series 61 and 62
Number of cylinders	V-8
Capacity (cubic inches)	331
Horsepower @ rpm	160 @ 3800
Transmission	3-speed manual or Hydra-matic
Maximum speed	100 mph
Acceleration 0-60 mph	13.4 seconds
Units produced	77,789
List price	$2,788 to $3,497

CHAPTER 8

TAIL FINS

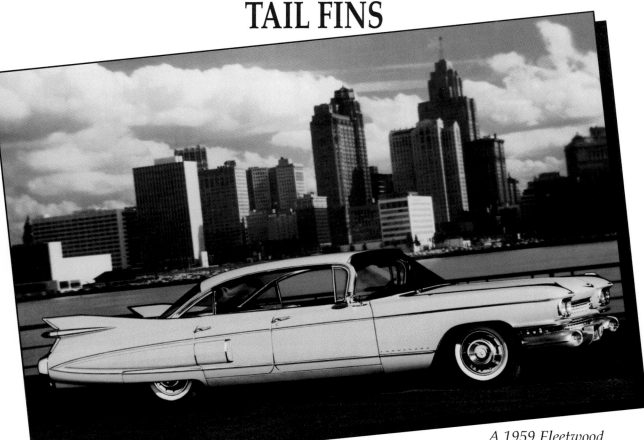

A 1959 Fleetwood 60 Special Sedan. This model more than any other shows the famous Cadillac "tail fins," one of the most remarkable design characteristics in the history of the motor car.

In 1948 Cadillac introduced one of the most famous and controversial automobile styling characteristics in the history of the motor car – the tail fin. The idea was adapted from a World War II airplane, Lockheed's P-38 fighter.

The idea was a stroke of styling genius. "Cad fins" had fantastic public appeal. Imitation fins were for sale in accessory shops all over the country. For just a few dollars, you could give your Chevy or Ford the "Caddie look."

In the early 1950s, the gas cap was hidden under the tail fin light. The light was hinged to raise when released by a concealed button.

As can be seen in the illustrations in this chapter, the size and predominance of the tail fins reached their peak with the 1959 model. After that year the fin was deliberately fazed out and today is nonexistent.

Model	1959 Series 62, 63, 60 Special, 64, 67, 69
Number of cylinders	V-8
Displacement (cubic inches)	390
Compression	10.5:1
Horsepower @ rpm	325 @ 4800
Maximum speed	117 mph
Acceleration 0-60 mph	11.2 seconds
Units produced	142,272
List price	$4,690 to $7,401

TAIL FINS THROUGH THE YEARS

1948

1950

1953

1954

1956

1957

1958

1959

1960

1961

1962

1963

1964

CHAPTER 9

CADILLAC, 1960-90

In the 1960s, '70s and '80s, Cadillac made some very attractive automobiles. Styling excesses of the late '50s were replaced with clean lines and more thoughtful, conservative designs. Buyers responded by purchasing Cadillacs in record-breaking numbers. Production increased from 142,184 cars in 1960 to 268,298 in 1990. This left no doubt as to what was America's favorite luxury car.

This "maturing" of the Cadillac image has cultural implications. Cars take on personalities and, like people, they assume a place in history. Cadillac is certainly remembered for its participation in celebrated events. Who could forget General Pershing in his Cadillac staff car in World War I; Al Capone in his 1930 armor-plated version (or J. Edgar Hoover in his); and J. Paul Getty, at a time when he was the richest man in the world, driving through the Communist Balkans in his "long shiny symbol of capitalist wealth." When President Nixon wanted to present Leonid Breshnev a token of goodwill, he gave him something American, a Cadillac. Celebrities, from Charles Lindbergh to the moon astronauts, are seen riding in parades in – what else? – a Cadillac. A car for a king or a president, a funeral or a rented limousine, is almost always a Cadillac.

A 1965 Eldorado Convertible. Long and lean, reduced tail fins, the luxury car of the '60s.

Model	1973 Calais, De Ville, Fleetwood
Number of cylinders	V-8
Displacement (cubic inches)	472
Compression	8.5:1
Horsepower @ rpm	345 @ 4400
Maximum speed	124 mph (estimated)
Acceleration 0-80 mph	17.6 seconds (estimated)
Units produced	253,315
List price	$5,886 to $12,080

A 1973 Fleetwood Eldorado Pace Car. A Cadillac convertible was the biggest and the best in the 1970s.

A 1980 Seville Elegante. The new "International" size Cadillac with bustle-back design.

CHAPTER 10

ALLANTÉ

In 1902, when the first Cadillac rolled out of a workshop on Trombley Avenue in Detroit, Michigan, it was distinguished by such luxury features as a steering wheel (other cars were steered by a tiller) and patent-leather mudguards over the wheels (the first fenders). In the late 1980s and early 1990s the company went to extraordinary lengths in pursuing the luxury-end of the business with an expensive two-door sports car, the Allanté.

Model	1993 Allanté
Engine	Northstar V-8, 32 valves
Displacement	4.6 liter
Compression	10.3:1
Horsepower @ rpm	295 @ 6000
Maximum speed	NA but more than 150 mph
Acceleration 0-60 mph	6.4 seconds (estimated)
List price	$62,500

The 1993 Allanté Convertible. The last model of an incredible car.

The plane that made the "world's longest assembly line" possible. A specially fitted Boeing 747 cargo plane ferried 56 car bodies per trip from Turin, Italy to Detroit's Metropolitan Airport, a distance of 3,300 miles.

By any standards, the Cadillac Allanté is a unique automobile. The body was designed and built in Italy by Pininfarina, the grand name of European coachbuilders. As with Lamborghini, Ferrari and other famous sports cars, the bodies were shipped from the coachbuilder to the automobile factory to be assembled with the chassis and power-train. But no other car manufacturers have ever done this from a distance of 3,300 miles.

The Allanté is an automobile of remarkable beauty with classic lines that are sure to be recorded in history as textbook examples of harmony and proportion. With the new Northstar engine, suspension and transmission, this car is a leader in engineering and technology. The Allanté goes like bullet and corners like a dream.

As this book is being written, Cadillac announced that Allanté production will end with the '93 model.

Cadillac general manager John O. Grettenberger showing how the Cadillac Allanté bodies were fitted into the plane with only an inch to spare. When Cadillac announced the "Airbridge" in 1987, the Allanté was the first American entry into the ultra-luxury automotive market.

CHAPTER 11

CADILLAC TODAY: DE VILLE, SIXTY SPECIAL, FLEETWOOD

The 1993 Sixty Special, a Cadillac name with a long tradition. The model was reintroduced into the 1993 product line as an upscale version of the De Ville. Cadillac calls the extra trim "a panache to the pampering."

A 1993 Fleetwood. This model is not just the biggest Cadillac, it is the largest four-door luxury automobile in standard production. And it is most likely the car from which more limousines are made than any other car in the world.

Model	1993 De Ville
Engine	V-8 with port fuel injection
Displacement	4.9 liter
Horsepower @ rpm	200 @ 4100
Maximum speed	NA but probably 120 mph
Acceleration 0-60 mph	9.0 seconds (estimated)
List price	$35,000

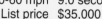

A 1993 Sedan De Ville. In the 1990s Cadillac expects to build over a quarter of a million cars each year. Over half of these, approximately 130,000 annually, will be the Sedan De Ville. It is America's leading four-door luxury car.

In the 1990s Cadillac finds itself more and more in a world market. The competition for luxury-class automobiles has escalated to frantic levels with the introduction of Japanese cars like Acura, Lexus and Infiniti. This greater contest for market share has made traditional European rivals also raise their marketing efforts to a feverish pitch. The situation is not unlike the 1930s, when famous cars like Duesenberg, Pierce-Arrow, Auburn, Marmon and Packard were fighting for survival. There may not be enough room for Mercedes, BMW, Jaguar, Lincoln *and* Cadillac. When your existence is threatened you work harder, and Cadillac Motor Car Division seems to be going flat-out to compete in the 1990s.

Why would someone buy a Cadillac rather than an expensive Japanese or European import? No single reason, but a few of the many might be as follows: better product quality, higher performance, better price, innovative features, better service, loyalty to American products and tradition.

All of this comes down to people. And the people at Cadillac have a lot going for them.

CHAPTER 12

CADILLAC TODAY:
SEVILLE AND ELDORADO

The 1992 Seville was named *Motor Trend* magazine's "Car of the Year." *Automobile Magazine* also chose it as "Automobile of the Year." *Car and Driver* listed it as one of "The Ten Best of 1992." The list could go on, but the bottom line is that the Seville STS was the first automobile to win every leading automotive magazine award. Quite an accomplishment, but the next year the Seville received a major improvement, the addition of the Northstar System. When the best gets better, you have a car of legendary quality.

Introduced in 1992 on the 1993 model Allanté, Northstar includes a 4.6 liter, 32-valve V-8 dual overhead camshaft (DOHC) engine. This new engine is a major technological achievement and

A 1993 Seville Touring Sedan. Cadillac's bid to compete with European and Japanese luxury cars is a very "peppy" car. The ride is reported to equal BMW's finest.

offers a number of engineering advances. Except for routine fluid replacement, the Northstar is designed to go a full 100,000 miles before its first scheduled tune-up. The engine is so quiet that a starter interlock is incorporated to prevent accidental starter engagement when the motor is running. The ignition is unique in that it contains no moving parts and is designed to supply consistent and uninterrupted spark up to 7000 rpm. All of this delivers impressive power and the best ratio of power to weight of any non-turbo engine in production.

To complete "the system" this new engine comes with an all new transmission and suspension. The transmission is operated by electronics rather than traditional hydraulic controls. The engine-transmission powertrain is managed by a computer that continually adjusts the operation to environmental factors.

The final component in the Northstar System is the suspension. It is fully independent, with variable-rate front springs; and short/long arm read design, with Cadillac's unique busing configuration and rear electronic level control.

The Northstar equipped Cadillac is the most "user friendly" of automobiles. It adapts itself to you. And if you put the pedal to the metal, it pops your neck.

A 1993 Eldorado. With the same chassis, same suspension, same basic design, there is no doubt this is the two-door cousin of the Seville. It should appeal to yuppie singles or couples who want a car with "punch."

Model	1993 Eldorado Touring Coupe
Engine	Northstar V-8, 32 valves
Displacement	4.6 liter
Compression	10.3:1
Horsepower @ rpm	295 @ 6000
Maximum speed	NA but more than 150 mph
Acceleration 0-60 mph	6.4 seconds (estimated)
List price	$40,000

CHAPTER 13

FUTURE CADILLACS

The photographs on this page give a layman's view of how Cadillac plans for the future. The general procedure is to take the best ideas of the car designers and engineers, and turn them into a concept car or show car.

Building concept cars is hardly new at Cadillac. In the 1950s, GM's chief stylist, Harley Earle, pioneered the idea of exhibiting concept cars at the major car shows. He monitored public reaction to new design ideas, saying, "It makes my job easier. By the time hundreds of thousands of these critics have examined your car at an exhibit, you have a firm idea of their likes and dislikes."

Concept cars also work in reverse and can aid the public in getting a preview of future vehicles. People who come to auto shows will identify with the product more easily when the production model reaches the street. An example of this was Cadillac's

Preliminary sketching of the concept car.

Final airbrushing on full-size, two-dimensional drawing.

Full-size clay model fitted with preliminary templates.

Final preparations are applied on clay model prior to making the car.

The car's interior is hand finished.

The completed concept car, ready for testing.

The only one of its kind, a Cadillac concept car on the road. It may be the Cadillac of the future.

concept car of the early 1980s, the Voyáge. It was equipped with a 4.5 liter, sequential-port, fuel-injected engine with traction control. A few years later, both features were standard equipment of the new Allanté.

This concept car features all-wheel-drive, four-passenger inflatable restraints and a sunroof that the driver can adjust automatically to darken. Will these become part of a Cadillac of the future?

CHAPTER 14

CADILLAC: IMPORTANT DATES

1902 The Detroit Automobile Company is reorganized and renamed the Cadillac Automobile Company. Henry Leland is a major stockholder.

1905 Cadillac is the pioneer of multi-cylinder motorcars, introducing the first 4-cylinder engine.

1908 Cadillac is the first American car to be awarded the Dewar Trophy by the Royal Automobile Club of London for being the first car to achieve interchangeability of parts.

1909 Cadillac is purchased by General Motors Corporation.

1913 Cadillac is the first company to equip cars with electric starting, lighting and ignition. The Royal Automobile Club awards a second Dewar Trophy.

1915 Cadillac is the first production car with a V-8, water-cooled engine.

1926 Cadillac is the first automaker to develop a comprehensive service policy and place it on a nationwide basis.

1928 Cadillac is the first to use the clashless synchromesh transmission.

1929 Cadillac is the first to offer laminated safety glass as standard equipment.

1930 Cadillac leads the development of a new V-16 engine.

1937 A Cadillac-built V-8 breaks all previous stock car records at the Indianapolis Speedway.

1942 Cadillac halts production of automobiles, produces tanks with Cadillac engines.

1945 On October 17 the first regular production car rolls off the line and begins the postwar era.

1948 Cadillac's chief designer, Harley Earle, changes the profile of all automobiles with the styling introduction of the tail fin.

1949 Introduction of the high compression, overhead valve V-8, the engine that changed the automobile industry.

1954 Cadillac is the first car manufacturer to provide power steering as standard equipment on its entire line of automobiles.

1970 Cadillac offers the largest production passenger car engine in the world, a 500 cubic inch (8.2 liter) V-8 on the Eldorado that delivers 400 horsepower.

1975 Cadillac is first to offer electronic fuel injection on an American vehicle.

1980 Cadillac advances fuel delivery technology with the introduction of digital electronic fuel injection, including self-diagnostics and microprocessor controls.

1985 Cadillac is the first production car manufacturer in the world to transverse-mount V-8 engines in a front-wheel drive configuration.

1987 Cadillac introduces the Allanté, America's first automobile to compete in the ultra-luxury segment of the market.

1992 Cadillac introduces the Northstar engine and suspension system.

1993 Northstar system becomes available on Seville and Eldorado.

GLOSSARY

Allanté – Cadillac's top-of-the-line sports car, introduced in 1987.

Cadillac (man) – The man who founded Detroit, Michigan in 1701. Full name is Le Sieur Antoine de la Mothe Cadillac.

Cadillac (auto) – The car manufactured by the Cadillac Motor Car Division of the General Motors Corporation.

chassis – The basic frame of the vehicle, on which all other parts are mounted.

DOHC – Dual overhead cam. Refers to two drives (instead of one) that operate the levers or cams that open and close the valves and are located over the head of the engine.

Leland – Henry Martyn Leland, the founder and first CEO of the Cadillac Automobile Company.

limousine – A large luxurious car, often driven by a chauffeur.

mph – Miles per hour. The speed of a car in miles per hour.

Northstar – The new high-performance engine, transmission and suspension system introduced by Cadillac in their 1993 models.

INDEX

Airbridge   23
Boeing 747   23
Cadillac, emblem   5
Cadillac, Le Sieur Antoine de la Mothe   5
Cadillac automobiles
    Allanté   22, 23, 26, 29
    Convertible, four-door, 1941   14
    Coupe, 1905   6
    Eldorado Biarritz Convertible, 1959   16
    Eldorado Convertible, 1965   20
    Eldorado Pace Car, 1973   21
    Eldorado, 1993   27
    Fleetwood, 1946   15
    Fleetwood, 1959   18
    Fleetwood, 1993   24
    Runabout, 1902   7
    Sedan De Ville, 1993   25
    Series 61 Convertible, 1949   17
    Series 62 Convertible, 1949   17
    Seville Elegante, 1980   21
    Seville STS, 1993   4, 26
    Sixty Special, 1993   18, 19, 24
    Touring Car, 1912   10
    V-16 Sport Phaeton, 1931   13
    Voyáge   29
Concept car   28, 29
DELCO   10, 11
Dewar Trophy   8, 10, 11
Earle, Harley   13, 28
Eggcrate grill   14
Electric starter   10, 11
Ford, Henry   6
General Motors   11
Grettenberger, John   23
Kettering, Charles F.   10, 11
Leland, Henry Martyn   6, 7
Lockheed P-38 fighter   18
Northstar System   22, 23, 26, 27
Pininfarina   23
Royal Automobile Club   8, 11
Tail fins   18, 19, 20
V-16   12, 13